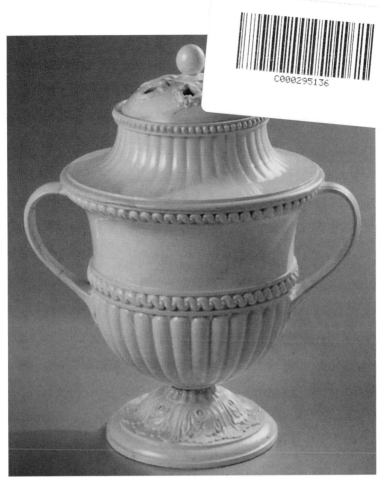

Cream-coloured earthenware pot-pourri vase, fluted and turned, c.1770. Height 318 mm. Unmarked.

WEDGWOOD WARE

Robert Copeland

A Shire book

Published in 2004 by Shire Publications Ltd, Cromwell House, Church Street, Princes Risborough, Buckinghamshire HP27 9AA, UK. Website: www.shirebooks.co.uk

British Library Cataloguing in Publication Data: Copeland, Robert. Wedgwood Ware. – 2nd ed. – (Shire album; 321) 1. Wedgwood Ware I. Title 738'.0942464. ISBN 0 7478 0612 8.

Cover: *(Back left) Handled vase in Black Basalt, on square plinth with moulded bands, c.1778; height 265 mm; wafer seal mark* WEDGWOOD & BENTLEY ETRURIA.
(Back centre) Tall handled vessel of lekythos form, Etruscan encaustic ware, with figure of a woman painted in red, c.1785; height 340 mm; mark WEDGWOOD *impressed.*
(Back right) Flower comport on foot, solid blue Jasper with applied strapwork decoration, c.1785; height 220 mm; impressed mark WEDGWOOD Z.
(Front left) Sauce tureen with fixed stand and cover in Queen's Ware with Green Water Leaf pattern painted on-glaze with gilded edge and traced handles, c.1775; length 222 mm; no mark.
(Front right) Bone china cream soup bowl and stand, 1959; black Asia pattern R4288; designed by Victor Skellern; diameter of stand 205 mm; mark WEDGWOOD BONE CHINA MADE IN ENGLAND.

Josiah Wedgwood FRS, 1730–95: roundel sculpted in marble by John Flaxman, c.1800.

Printed in Great Britain by CIT Printing Services Ltd, Press Buildings, Merlins Bridge, Haverfordwest, Pembrokeshire SA61 1XF.

CONTENTS

Earthenware vase, 1863, height 1.5 metres. Decorated by Emile Lessore with the subject 'The Defeat of Porus', after a series of paintings by Charles le Brun.

Cream-coloured earthenware teapot moulded with a panel representing a pineapple, probably modelled by William Greatbatch. Leaf area, handle, knob and tip of spout glazed in green, the rest in yellow. Staffordshire, c.1765–70. Unmarked.

THE EARLY YEARS, 1730–66

Josiah Wedgwood I was born in 1730 and was baptised on 12th July at St John's Church, Burslem, North Staffordshire. His parents were Thomas Wedgwood III and Mary, née Stringer. Thomas was the third member of the family to own the Churchyard Works in Burslem, and on his death in 1739 he left it to his eldest son, Thomas. It is thought that young Josiah, at the age of nine, left school to work for his brother at the family works. In his youth he contracted smallpox and, although he recovered, his right knee was rendered extremely stiff with a complaint known as Brodie's abscess, so that his movements were seriously hampered.

The throwing room (in the Ornamental Works) at Etruria. This would have been not much different from throwing rooms in other manufactories of the eighteenth century.

4

The Brick House (Bell Works): a modern line drawing after a nineteenth-century engraving. It illustrates the typical characteristics of a Staffordshire potbank: bottle ovens, yard and outside steps.

When he was fourteen years old he was apprenticed to his brother Thomas. The principal method of making hollow pots in those days was by 'throwing' on a wheel rotating horizontally on a vertical shaft. It is known that Josiah learnt this particular craft: by the time his apprenticeship ended in about 1749 he would have grasped thoroughly all the best practices of potting.

After a partnership with Harrison and Alders in Stoke-upon-Trent from 1752 to 1754, he entered into another in 1754 with the leading manufacturer of earthenware, Thomas Whieldon. Here he would have met William Greatbatch and also Josiah Spode, three years his junior, just as Spode ended his five-year apprenticeship. While he was with Whieldon in Fenton Vivian, Wedgwood experimented, especially with glaze effects, one of which he recorded in an experiment book on 23rd March 1759: 'A Green Glaze, to be laid on common white (or Cream color) Bis cuit [sic] ware. Very good.'

He left this fruitful partnership in 1759, returned to Burslem and commenced potting on his own account in factories he rented from his kinsmen, John and Thomas Wedgwood. His business flourished to such an extent that he moved to another pottery works in Burslem, called the Brick House. Above this he built a cupola for a bell that was tolled to summon his employees to work (instead of blowing a horn); so the factory became known as the Bell Works. From simple unmoulded items he expanded his range of products to include teapots and other objects in the form of natural subjects, such as 'melon sauce boats and stands'. The models and moulds were made for him by William Greatbatch, who had been a fellow worker at Whieldon's manufactory. The Whieldon-Wedgwood range had included teapots and coffee pots in the shape of pineapples, cauliflowers and other items, and Wedgwood probably continued the same or similar ranges when he returned to Burslem.

Cream-coloured earthenware cream jug of melon type with green and yellow glazes, c.1770. Unmarked. (St Louis Art Museum.)

5

Cream-coloured earthenware teapot of cauliflower form decorated with green glaze, c.1760–5. Height 134 mm. Unmarked.

It is believed that Enoch Booth, in about 1740, was the first potter to make 'cream-coloured' earthenware. This is a twice-fired product. The body, of plastic 'ball' clay and ground flint, was shaped and then fired without being glazed, at about 1150°C (2100°F) to yield a 'biscuit' pot. Then glaze, a mixture of glass-forming ingredients, was applied to the pot, which was refired at a temperature about 100°C lower than the biscuit fire. Whieldon, Wedgwood and other potters followed Booth, but they mostly used glazes coloured with mineral oxides to give greens, browns and yellows. True 'creamware' has a plain cream colour which is caused by traces of iron in the lead-based glaze. Examples of painted teapots and other objects are known.

Wedgwood carried out many experiments in order to regularise the recipes both of the clay mixings and of the cream-coloured glaze. By about 1762 he was satisfied that he had achieved the desired result, and original and elegant designs were developed which excited his customers. Some of his tablewares were designed to suit the neo-classical interiors that were becoming the vogue in the houses of the well-to-do.

He sent some of this ware to Liverpool to be printed by John Sadler and Guy Green, who in 1756 had perfected the method of printing by transferring the images from engraved copper plates to the glazed surface of the pottery objects. Various subjects were printed, in black, red or purple.

On his journeys to Liverpool Wedgwood saw for himself how bad

Tray of cream-coloured earthenware tablets – trials used to perfect the ceramic body which by the early 1760s was known as Queen's Ware.

6

Queen's Ware helmet-shape ewer with 'Brown Broad and Fine Line' pattern as decoration, c.1775. Height 254 mm.

the roads were: in bad weather they were almost impassable. He promoted the development of a paved turnpike road through Burslem to join that from London to Liverpool and to be paid for by tolls collected from those who used it. Although local town traders objected to potential passing trade being diverted, the road bypassed Newcastle-under-Lyme and cut the journey by 4 miles (6 km). From 1763 this road made easier the passage of carts and packhorses to Liverpool and to the salt-wyches of Cheshire, which supplied the important ingredient for salt-glazing pottery.

On one visit to Liverpool in 1762 Josiah was thrown from his horse and injured his already damaged right leg. While he rested, the local surgeon, Matthew Turner, brought his friend Thomas Bentley to keep Josiah company. From this meeting grew a fine and profitable friendship and partnership. Bentley's views on religion and politics were similar to Wedgwood's, but Bentley was better educated and he had a wider experience as a merchant.

The growing fashion for drinking coffee, hot chocolate and, more recently, tea enlarged the market for cups, saucers and other vessels needed for their enjoyment. In 1765 Queen Charlotte ordered 'A complete sett of tea things, with a gold ground & raised flowers upon it in green'. It was for twelve people. Although many potters had had the opportunity to tender for this order, only Wedgwood saw the advantage of doing so. In the following year the firm supplied the

Queen's Ware plate with feather edge and pierced border and central scene of 'Corinthian Ruins', transfer-printed in purple, c.1775; diameter 230 mm. Queen's Ware teapot with ball finial and leafage spout, decorated with a Sadler & Green print of 'The Death of Wolfe' (from the engraving by William Woollett after the painting by Benjamin West) and the framed inscription 'Success to the INDEPENDENT VOLUNTEER SOCIETIES of the Kingdom of IRELAND. FOR MY COUNTRY', c.1775; height 165 mm.

7

Portrait of Thomas Bentley (1730–80), partner of Josiah Wedgwood I in the Ornamental Works, 1769–80; oil on canvas, after John Francis Rigaud (1742–1810).

Queen with a table service and in that summer Wedgwood was appointed (or at least was permitted to use the title of) 'Potter to Her Majesty', and his creamware became known as Queen's Ware, a name that carried great prestige both in Britain and abroad.

Perfecting his creamware was possibly Wedgwood's greatest contribution to the repertoire of the pottery industry. It was useful, attractive and hygienic, easy to make and fairly priced so that it could be afforded by both the wealthy and middle classes.

Wedgwood realised that it was important to have a showroom in London to show his ware to the nobility. In 1765 he rented two rooms in Cateaton Street at the Sign of the Artichoke, but he swiftly moved to another rented showroom in Charles Street, Grosvenor Square, in 1766.

He set out to capture the world of fashion, stating that 'Fashion is infinitely superior to merit in many respects'. The continuing increase in tea drinking led to a growing demand for earthenware, and the increase in population meant a growing market with expanding needs. His selling policy was first to seek the patronage of the nobility and figures well-known in fashionable and artistic circles, and he started by choosing the Queen as his sponsor. He said: '...begin at the Head first, and then proceed to the inferior members.'

When the demand for Queen's Ware was more than he could meet Wedgwood completed orders with the best the manufacturers around him could supply. It is thought that he arranged for some of them to manufacture to his specifications and to keep the ware in their own warehouses until he called it forward to fulfil orders; these warehouses he called

Plate 7 from the 'Useful Ware' (Queen's Ware) catalogue of 1774, featuring dinnerware items and an egg cup.

8

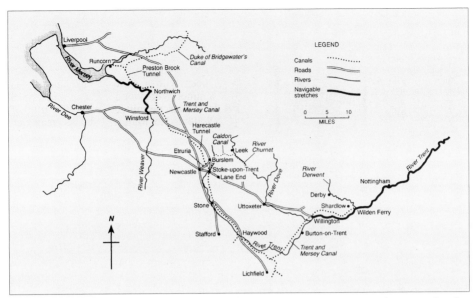

Plan of the Grand Trunk Canal from the river Trent to the river Mersey. The canal was completed in 1777.

his 'banks', and it seems likely that this is the origin of the term 'potbank' to refer to a pottery works.

Wedgwood saw the need to link the river Trent with the river Mersey and not only raised finance but won political support in Parliament through the influence of landowners like Earl Gower and the Duke of Bridgewater. He gave a lead by himself investing in the scheme and he was appointed treasurer of 'The Proprietors of the Navigation between the Trent & the Mersey', who included the Duke of Bridgewater, Earl Gower (from Trentham), Thomas Anson (from Shugborough), Mr Bagot and many local landowners, merchants and manufacturers. On 26th July 1766 he dug the first sod to inaugurate the construction. His knowledge of the route of the canal must have influenced his purchase in that year of the Ridge House Estate of 350 acres (142 hectares) on which he would build his new manufactory and residence.

Josiah Wedgwood I's original engine-turning lathe in situ at the old Etruria Works. Tom Simpson is seen here working on a fluted Jasper vase in about 1933.

THE DECADE OF DEVELOPMENTS, 1767–77

Wedgwood bought the site for his new manufactory in December 1767. In the summer of that year Wedgwood and Bentley had agreed to become partners in the new works, to be called Etruria, named in recognition of the discoveries made in Pompeii and Herculaneum.

In 1763 Wedgwood had introduced to the industry the 'dicing' lathe, which incised chequer designs on pots, and during 1767 the development of the 'rose' engine-turning lathe was completed. This ingenious lathe enabled not only the usual chequered effect to be made but also the parallel vertical stripes that are important features of many of Wedgwood's neo-classical vases and other hollow wares. John Wyke of Liverpool made the improvements and the original lathe is preserved in the Wedgwood Museum at Barlaston; it is still used occasionally.

In May 1768 the condition of Josiah's right leg deteriorated so badly that it was amputated above the knee. That this proved

The old treadle lathe at Etruria: drawing by James Hodgkiss, 1919, reproduced from 'Artes Etruriae Renascuntur', 1920.

10

a satisfactory operation is a great credit to the surgeon and to Josiah's fortitude.

It was to manufacture vases in Black Basalt that the first section of the works was built at Etruria and in the late summer of 1768 the first successful ones were made. Wedgwood adopted the name 'Basaltes' in 1773 for what had up to then been called 'Egyptian black ware', which was the earlier unrefined black dry stoneware made by several potters. The first section of the Etruria Works was opened on 13th June 1769. To mark this great event, six 'First Day's Vases' were thrown on the wheel by Josiah Wedgwood while Thomas Bentley turned the crank of the great wheel. These vases were decorated and inscribed in the style called 'Encaustic'. This was a Black Basalt body with the ornamentation painted on the surface in oxides of iron, which, on being fired in the decorating kiln, fused with the body and remained matt to give the appearance of actual red clay.

At the same time Wedgwood heeded the advice of some members of the nobility by opening a showroom at Number 1, Great Newport Street, Soho, in London in 1768. In August 1769 Thomas Bentley moved to London to oversee it.

'Porkoipin for snowdrips' (sic): hedgehog bulb pot for snowdrops. Black Basalt, c.1775.

11

First Day's Vases: two of six thrown by Josiah Wedgwood to commemorate the opening of his Etruria manufactory on 13th June 1769. Encaustic decorated in iron red enamels on the Black Basalt body with a scene taken from 'A Collection of Etruscan, Greek and Roman Antiquities from the Cabinet of the Hon'ble William Hamilton, 1766–67' by d'Hancarville, volume I, plate 129. The factory motto, 'Artes Etruriae Renascuntur', is visible. Height 254 mm. Unmarked.

Cream-coloured earthenware vase (left) with surface decoration of coloured glazes, to emulate the appearance of agate, and twisted snakes as handles, c.1775. Mark on base Wedgwood & Bentley. Creamware vase (right), shape number 1, the surface decorated with stippled colours to emulate porphyry and satyrs' masks with horns as handles, c.1770–5. Height 406 mm. Mark on Black Basalt base WEDGWOOD & BENTLEY impressed in a circle on a thin pad of applied clay.

Left: *Black Basalt vase, engine turning to main body, leopards' heads as handles. Laurel border (overlapping) at the base of the neck of the vase. Height 432 mm.* WEDGWOOD & BENTLEY *wafer seal mark, c.1775.*

Below: *Two Black Basalt busts portraying Germanicus (left) and Marcus Aurelius (right). Height of 'Germanicus' 457 mm. The library bust of 'Marcus Aurelius' features the* WEDGWOOD & BENTLEY *mark impressed in two places. Both pieces c.1775–80.*

Below: *Black Basalt cream jug and cup and saucer, with hand-painted 'Running Anthemion' border in red and white encaustic enamels. Creamer 89 mm high, teacup and saucer impressed* WEDGWOOD; *creamer impressed* WEDGWOOD & BENTLEY, *c.1772.*

13

At this time Wedgwood began to produce creamware effects described as 'marbled' and 'porphyry'. The former was achieved by intermingling clay slips of different colours on the surface of a clay pot, the latter by sprinkling different coloured mineral powders on to the damp surface of a creamware biscuit pot and then covering it with a lead glaze to yield a powdered effect similar to natural stone.

The classical form of all Wedgwood's vases admirably suited the elegance of the new well-proportioned Georgian interiors, but

Modern line drawing of the Etruria Works, after an original mid nineteenth-century woodcut. A horse-drawn narrowboat is seen on the Trent & Mersey Canal in the foreground.

Wedgwood wrote in 1770: 'I never had any idea that the Ornamental ware should not be of some use.'

The length of the Grand Trunk Canal from Stone to Shardlow on the river Trent was completed by 1772, and until the canal reached Etruria in 1773 Wedgwood sent his products to Stone for shipment on the narrowboats. The canal was not opened along its complete length of 93 miles (150 km) until 1777 because engineering difficulties were encountered in tunnelling through Harecastle Hill and Preston Hill. By this canal 'inland transport was reduced one fourth in cost': for example, the cost per ton by road between Liverpool and Etruria in August 1777 was £2 10s 0d and by water 13s 4d. In a letter of 13th February 1786 to R. L. Edgworth, Wedgwood stated that freight costs were reduced from 10d per ton per mile to $1\frac{1}{2}$d per ton per mile.

14

Creamware oval lobed dessert dish, shape number 1318, hand-enamelled in puce with the 'Husk Border' and floral centre, c.1770. 292 by 216 mm.

In 1768 Lord Cathcart was appointed Ambassador Extraordinary to the court of the Empress Catherine the Great of Russia. He ordered a crested dinner and dessert service for himself from Wedgwood. Characteristically Josiah seized the opportunity thus presented to discuss ways in which Lord Cathcart could help to promote trade – especially Wedgwood's – between the two countries. It was primarily Lady Cathcart who had the Empress's attention at court. In 1770 the Empress ordered a dinner service decorated with flowers painted in mulberry,

Queen's Ware dessert plate painted in monochrome, with laurel border and green enamel frog crest and central 'View on the Thames near Isleworth, Middlesex', c.1774. Diameter 241 mm. Unmarked.

15

and in 1773 Wedgwood began to negotiate with the British consul, Alexander Baxter, acting for the Empress, to supply a large table service of nearly one thousand pieces, each to be painted in sepia with a scene of a different, named English house or landscape and to bear the crest of a frog in a panel in the border, because the service was for use in the Chesmenski Palace, which was in an area called La Grenouilliere, or Frog-marsh. The service was completed in the following year – an astonishing achievement – and was warmly approved of by the Empress. It was the most important service ever made in earthenware by an English manufacturer.

All Wedgwood's goods were much more expensive than those of his contemporaries. He decided not to compete on price because 'low prices beget low quality in the manufacture, which will beget contempt'. He chose not to charge what an object was worth but a price that the nobility would pay for it. In order to stay ahead of his rivals, many of whom were quick to copy his wares, Wedgwood adopted sophisticated techniques of selling. He appealed to the fashionable call for antiquities, he paid attention to the excitement over the discoveries at Pompeii and Herculaneum, and he provided for the ceramic desires of the wealthy. He asked their advice, he accepted small special orders, he flattered them and made his London showroom especially attractive to the ladies. So they praised, endorsed and bought his ware. Their lead was followed by other members of their class who could afford to. He saw the importance of names: Queen's Ware, Royal shape, Devonshire flowerpots, etc. His showroom displays were changed every few days so that Wedgwood's became one of the most fashionable meeting places in London and regular visitors could always see some new attraction. He used showrooms, warehouses, trademarks, 'puffing articles' and advertisements, to keep up the pressure.

Trade increased and in 1774 Wedgwood leased premises in Portland House, Greek Street, London, from the Duke of Portland, to replace the showroom in Great Newport Street. The painting workshop in Chelsea, which had become operational in 1769, and where the service for Empress Catherine was decorated, also moved there. Bentley lived nearby, so he was able to oversee the departments which were now all close at hand.

Bentley urged Wedgwood to add a dry red stoneware body to the range. Wedgwood did so reluctantly because, as he said, 'it puts you in mind of a red pot teapot'. Despite this, it suited his love of the classical, so it is not surprising that he called this ware 'Rosso Antico'.

In 1775 Wedgwood led a group of Staffordshire potters in opposing the extension of the patent owned by Richard

Rosso Antico pot-pourri vase with pierced cover and moulded basket-weave effect, with Egyptian-inspired reliefs in Black Basalt, c.1790. Height 242 mm. Impressed mark WEDGWOOD.

16

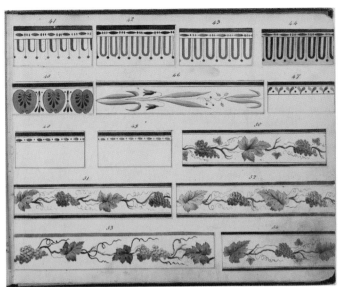

Wedgwood's first pattern book, featuring border pattern numbers 41 to 54 inclusive.

Champion for the exclusive manufacture of true hardpaste porcelain and of his monopoly of the use of china clay and Cornish stone. While the patent for true porcelain was extended by Parliament for fourteen years until 1796, the monopoly of the use of china clay and Cornish stone was broken. Their use by others was permitted provided that Champion's specification for porcelain was not infringed. This concession was a major victory for Wedgwood and his supporters because it meant that not only could experiments in improving porcelain take place but also that these essential materials were available for the improvement of earthenware and the development of fine stoneware bodies. Shortly after the bill received the Royal Assent, Wedgwood went to Cornwall with John Turner and Thomas Griffiths to secure a supply of these materials. Once again, Wedgwood had pioneered a course of action in his own interest that opened up huge opportunities for the whole industry. This was true also of the introduction of Jasper, of

Oval plaque in solid blue and white Jasper, the bas-relief depicting 'The Judgement of Hercules', c.1777. Modelled by William Hackwood. Ormolu frame, with ribbon tie loop. 254 by 330 mm. Impressed mark WEDGWOOD & BENTLEY.

17

Helmet-shape cream jug (left) (height 100 mm) and (right) low cream jug (height 72 mm) of white Jasper, blue dip, with relief sprigged decoration and engine-turned lower part of body, c.1785.

whiter and stronger earthenwares and, for other potters to develop in later years, fine bone china and stone china.

Wedgwood's big success in 1774 was at last to achieve a satisfactory stoneware in which to manufacture cameos, vases and utilitarian objects. The cameo form was of a white bas-relief on a coloured body. Wedgwood had studied the jewellery and decorative arts of the ancients and realised that there was great interest in antique cameos, which were made of natural stone or of glass. He decided to try to manufacture contemporary cameos of white on a coloured opaque background and he called his product 'Jasper'. The principal ingredient was barytes (barium sulphate), or cawk. This yielded a fine-grained white stoneware for the 'sprigs'

Coffee pot and cover of white Jasper, blue dip, engine-turned base and cover, with relief sprigged decoration, 1783–90. Height 215 mm. Impressed mark WEDGWOOD 3.

18

Teapot of Empire shape, blue Jasper, white bas-relief of Charlotte at the tomb of Werther. Engine-turned decoration at base and on cover; c.1785. Impressed Wedgwood.

or bas-reliefs, and these he applied to small background tablets which he coloured blue with a cobalt stain.

This blue Jasper has become Wedgwood's most famous product and was of a very fine smooth texture. To achieve it, Wedgwood carried out several thousand recorded trials before he was satisfied. In one formula both china clay and Cornish stone were important ingredients, so his fight against Champion and visit to Cornwall were crucial to his experiments. Several types of blue Jasper were made: some had just a 'blue dip' because the cost of the cobalt was so high; another, solid Jasper, had the blue colour throughout the entire medium. There were also sea-green, lilac and other colours. However, there continued to be many problems to be overcome, and it was several years before Wedgwood felt that he had solved them all. The Jasper reliefs, formed in delicately made moulds, displayed very sharp detail and, because no glaze was necessary, this detail was not blurred.

White on pale blue Jasper 'Venus', also known as the 'snake-handled' vase. The bas-relief ornament depicts 'Venus in her Chariot drawn by swans', which was adapted from the work of Charles le Brun. Height 419 mm. Impressed WEDGWOOD, *c.1785.*

19

Cane Ware game-pie dish with glazed inner lining, rabbit finial and 'Dead Game' as reliefs, nineteenth century. 242 by 165 mm. Impressed WEDGWOOD. *Game-pie dishes had been suggested to Wedgwood by Richard Edgworth as early as 1786.*

In the early 1770s a buff-coloured dry stoneware body called 'Cane Ware' was developed. In later years, during the wars with the French Republic, this body was used to imitate the pie-crust when grain was in short supply. Casserole dishes and covers, glazed inside for easy cleaning, were popular. Dessert services in the form of different shapes of shells were considered attractive, sometimes edged with a green enamel line.

Group of ware made for scientific purposes, including a mortar and pestle, rectangular 'fossil' cups, two crucibles (in front) and three oval evaporating pans, c.1780–5. Length of pestle with handle 152 mm. Marks, various.

CONSOLIDATION OF THE BUSINESS

The painter George Stubbs asked Wedgwood in 1775 to make large slabs of earthenware on which he wished to paint in enamel colours. He had been painting on sheets of copper, which were smoother than canvas, and the colours, being fired on, did not fade, but copper sheets larger than 18 by 15 inches (457 by 381 mm) buckled in the fire. After much effort oval slabs, or tablets, as large as 30 by 40 inches (762 by 1016 mm) were supplied.

In 1779 Wedgwood launched his 'Pearl Ware' to sell beside Queen's Ware. This is a similar biscuit ware to creamware but with a cobalt blue stain added to the glaze to offset the yellow effect caused by iron. This produced a pale grey colour. Where the glaze gathers, such as by the foot-rings, a distinct blueness may be seen. In the nineteenth century it was widely used for transfer-printed blue patterns.

Wedgwood began to make articles for scientific use by chemists and scientists. He perfected a ceramic body in which he made heat-resistant crucibles, retorts and other vessels; a most important development in 1779 was the mortar stoneware body for pestles

Pearl Ware tankard, featuring an underglaze blue-printed design known as 'Water Lily', c.1811. Height 127 mm. Impressed WEDGWOOD.

Portrait of Dr Erasmus Darwin, a Wedgwood biscuit earthenware plaque. 660 by 521 mm. Inscribed 'Geo. Stubbs Pinxit 1783'.

Cream-coloured earthenware whisky still, c.1785– 90. Height 440 mm. (Colonial Williamsburg Collection, Williamsburg, Virginia.)

and mortars. He was a member of the Lunar Society in Birmingham and he was very friendly with Joseph Priestley, who discovered oxygen, to whom he gave money and chemical ware from time to time. Matthew Boulton, James Watt, Dr Erasmus Darwin and others were his friends too.

Sir William Hamilton, Plenipotentiary in Naples, was a serious collector of antique Greek vases, and his collection had been drawn and the illustrations published in 1766–7. Some of these had inspired Wedgwood's Black Basalt wares. In 1778 Wedgwood sent a present to Sir William of a Jasper tablet of 'The Apotheosis of Homer' and Hamilton suggested other subjects for Wedgwood to adapt.

Wedgwood was always seeking the best talent for his purposes and with the rapid success of his Black Basalt and blue Jasper he needed skilled modellers, especially of figures and portrait cameos. The sculptor John Flaxman junior worked for Wedgwood from 1775, modelling portraits and bas-reliefs of antique subjects. William Hackwood was engaged in 1769 and worked at Etruria for sixty-three years. He became known, among other things, for his Jasper medallion of a kneeling slave in chains, with the inscription 'Am I not a man and a brother?', which he modelled in 1787.

22

Thomas Bentley died on 26th November 1780 at the age of fifty. This was a serious blow to Josiah, who had confided in him and leant on him for his advice since they had met in Liverpool. The stock of goods held jointly by the two partners was sold by auction in December 1781. So ended the fruitful partnership of Wedgwood and Bentley, which had begun in 1769 with the opening of the Etruria Works. Thomas Byerley, Josiah's nephew, was sent to London to take charge of the business there.

In 1782 Wedgwood decided to install a steam engine to power his grinding mill. Josiah Spode had installed one in 1779, so a note was sent to the engineer James Watt giving details of the arrangement of Spode's engine. It was a steam pumping engine of the Newcomen type, which pumped water to a tank on the upper floor of the building, from where the water flowed to an overshot waterwheel, which was geared to the vertical shaft of the grinding pan. For

Right: *Lidded vase of white Jasper, mid-blue dip with white bas-relief of 'The Apotheosis of Homer' and Pegasus (winged horse) finial. The relief was modelled in 1778 by John Flaxman junior (1755–1826); the vase form, also modelled by him, appeared in 1786. Height 458 mm. Impressed mark* WEDGWOOD. *This example dates from the early nineteenth century.*

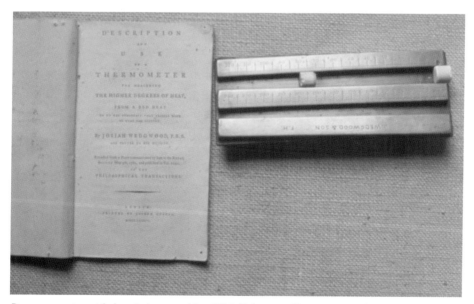

Brass pyrometer with descriptive pamphlet, 1784. Title page: 'Description and Use of a Thermometer for Measuring the Higher Degrees of Heat, from a red heat up to the strongest that vessels made of clay can support'.

Copy of the famous cameo glass Portland (Barberini) Vase, now in the British Museum. In white on black Jasper, this fine example is from the first edition begun by Josiah I in October 1789 and once belonged to the famous antiquarian Thomas Hope. Height 254 mm. Unmarked.

Wedgwood, however, Watt provided in 1784 a more advanced engine which drove a flywheel, so giving direct rotative motion.

After years of experiment Wedgwood found a more accurate method of determining the heat inside a kiln. For this advance in pyrometry and contribution to science he was elected a Fellow of the Royal Society in 1783.

Until 1784 Wedgwood had sent his ware to Liverpool to be printed but in that year he began to print on-glaze in small quantities at Etruria. However, when in that same year transfer-printing in blue under the glaze on earthenware was perfected by Josiah Spode, Wedgwood's painters 'waited upon Mr Wedgwood to solicit his influence in preventing its establishment'. Wedgwood kept his promise 'not to make it' in his lifetime and so lost the valuable blue and white trade.

In 1784 Sir William Hamilton brought to England a unique first-century vase that he had acquired in Italy. Then known as the Barberini Vase, it was of dark blue glass, overlaid with opaque thin white glass carved into figures. Hamilton sold it to the Duchess of Portland, and it has since been known as the Portland Vase. The Duchess died shortly after and the vase was bought at the auction of her effects by her son, the third Duke of Portland. He lent it in 1786 to Wedgwood to copy. By October 1789 Wedgwood had succeeded in producing a replica in black and white Jasper and a copy was exhibited at the Greek Street showrooms in April and May 1790.

Josiah had married his cousin, Sarah Wedgwood, in January 1764. They had eight children. In 1790 three sons, John, Josiah II and

Thomas, were made partners in the business, which became Wedgwood, Sons & Byerley. John and Tom were not interested in becoming potters and relinquished their partnerships in 1793. Josiah by then was in semi-retirement, and he died on 3rd January 1795.

His memorial plaque in the church of St Peter ad Vincula in Stoke-upon-Trent states that he 'converted a rude and inconsiderable Manufactory into an elegant Art and an important part of the National Commerce'. Although the industry into which he was born was not all that rude and inconsiderable for the time, there is no doubt that Josiah Wedgwood was the most important potter Britain has produced.

Josiah Wedgwood's memorial in the church of St Peter ad Vincula, Stoke-upon-Trent. The inscription reads:

'Sacred to the memory of Josiah Wedgwood FRS & SA of Etruria in this county. Born in August [sic] 1730. Died January the 3rd 1795. Who converted a rude & inconsiderable manufactory into an elegant art and an important part of national commerce. By these services to his country he acquired an ample fortune which he blamelessly & reasonably enjoyed and generously dispensed for the reward of merit & the relief of misfortune. His mind was inventive & original yet perfectly sober & well regulated. His character was decisive & commanding without rashness or arrogance. His probity was inflexible, his kindness unwearied. His manners simple & dignified and the chearfulness [sic] of his temper was the natural reward of the activity of his pure & useful life. He was most loved by those who knew him best and he has left indelible impressions of affection & veneration on the minds of his family who have erected this monument to his memory.'

25

Earthenware dessert plate, shell-shaped with variegated lustre, c.1810. Diameter at widest point 229 mm. Impressed mark WEDGWOOD.

THE NINETEENTH CENTURY

Josiah Wedgwood died a very rich man, with total wealth of about £500,000. He left much of this to his children, but unfortunately none of the sons showed much interest in the business. Josiah II inherited the Etruria estate, Etruria Hall and the manufactory, but four months after his father's death he moved to Surrey, and later to Dorset, returning to Staffordshire in 1807. It was left to Thomas Byerley to shoulder the burden on his own. The London showroom was moved to York Street, St James's. Trade was difficult because of the protracted war against Napoleon. John Wedgwood rejoined as a partner in 1800.

Various metallic lustres were made, including the 'variegated' lustre which was much admired. A second Watt steam engine was installed in 1801 and this was used to drive pottery-making machinery like throwing wheels and turning lathes. It ran until 1912.

When John Wedgwood took up residence in North Staffordshire in 1804, he found utter confusion and deterioration at Etruria. Kiln losses were high and he took firm measures which resulted in improvements. By the end of 1805 under-glaze transfer-printed patterns were being marketed in

Portrait of Josiah Wedgwood II MP (1769–1843), second son of Josiah I: oil on canvas by William Owen RA.

26

Rotative steam engine by Boulton & Watt installed at Etruria in 1801 and in use until 1912.

order to meet the competition from firms like Spode, Rogers, Riley, Ridgway, Davenport and Minton. Several attractive patterns were produced in the following years.

Thomas Byerley died on 11th September 1810 and he was succeeded in London by his son, Josiah.

In 1812, probably because of the success which attended Spode's introduction and marketing of bone china, and because earthenware was now less fashionable, Wedgwood adopted the manufacture of bone china using a formula similar to that of other makers. It was launched in a rather half-hearted manner and full production ceased in about 1823, although orders continued to be supplied up to 1829, when the London showroom was closed.

A stone china body was made from 1820 to about 1825 or even later. This, like bone china, was adopted because of the pressure of competition. Stone china was a pale grey vitreous feldspathic earthenware made to match the colour of Chinese export porcelain.

Francis Wedgwood (1800–88), Josiah II's third son, was made a partner in 1827 and immediately set about rejuvenating the whole business. Josiah II died on 12th July 1843 and four months later

Below left: *Earthenware plate, transfer-printed in blue under-glaze, 'Hibiscus' pattern, 1806. Diameter 240 mm.*

Below right: *Earthenware plate, transfer-printed in blue under-glaze, 'Peony' pattern, 1807. Diameter 240 mm.*

Portrait medallion of Thomas Byerley (1742–1810), nephew of Josiah I and partner in the firm from 1790 to 1810; white Jasper, dark blue dip. Modelled by William Theed in 1810.

Francis took several partners, including his own three sons. At the Great Exhibition of 1851 the firm mounted a large display, which included many examples of Jasper and of the recently adopted statuary porcelain (Parian), which Wedgwood called 'Carrara'. A Prize Medal was awarded by the jury.

Although reproductions of past products continued to form an important part of the range, the firm needed to move forward and compete with the leading manufacturers. A new product introduced by Minton was called 'Majolica'. This was an earthenware body, exuberantly modelled into natural forms and decorated with coloured, translucent and opaque lead glazes. It was inspired by but totally different from the Italian tin-glazed *maiolica* of the fifteenth and sixteenth centuries. Wedgwood adopted the idea in 1860.

In 1858 the French painter Emile Lessore joined Wedgwood and, in his inimitable style of semi-impressionist genre subjects of figures in landscapes, decorated very many ornamental wares. He soon decided to live in London in the summer and in France in the winter, where Wedgwood sent ware out to him for decoration.

Group of first-period bone china teaware, c.1813, hand-painted with pictorial views by John Cutts, some views named on the base, gilded edge lines with some gilding to finials. Height of teapot 152 mm. Mark WEDGWOOD, *printed in red.*

28

Group of first-period bone china teaware, c.1815, gilded edge lines and some gilding to finials, spout and base of spout. Height of teapot 152 mm. Mark WEDGWOOD *in red.*

New designs for artwares began to appear in 1865, produced by Christopher Dresser and Walter Crane. The employment of these freelance designers established what became a tradition at Wedgwood, although they continued to engage full-time designers such as Harry

Pearl Ware ewer and mug, under-glaze blue printed pattern of the so-called 'Darwin Water Lily', c.1811. Both impressed WEDGWOOD.

An old photograph from the archive of the Etruria Works, c.1870–80, of figures in Carrara porcelain, or Parian. From left: 'The Wanderer' by E. Shenton, 1859, height 457 mm; 'The Sacrifice' (the angel preventing Abraham from offering up his son, Isaac), sculpted by W. Beattie, height 610 mm; 'Milton', height 445 mm.

Pair of Majolica dolphin candlesticks inspired by an early model of 1800. Impressed WEDGWOOD. Date c.1860.

Queen's Ware teapot, 'Satsuma' shape, with domestic scene hand-painted by Emile Lessore, c.1862. Height 133 mm. Impressed mark WEDGWOOD *and indistinct date code.*

Right: *Earthenware spill vase, decorated with a printed and gilded pattern by Christopher Dresser. The design was registered originally in 1867. Height 260 mm. Impressed mark* WEDGWOOD.

Below: *Pair of Queen's Ware vases, decorated with figures representing the arts of painting and music, designed by Walter Crane. Height 197 mm. Impressed mark* WEDGWOOD *and date mark WUQ for 1888.*

31

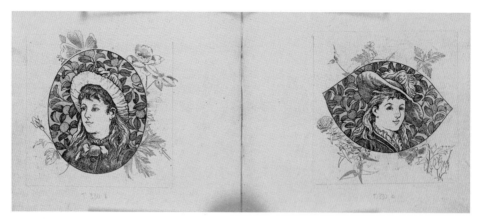

Page from the tile pattern books showing two of the four 'Cameo Heads' designed c.1883 by Thomas Allen, art director at Etruria. These designs appeared on 6 inch (152 mm) and 8 inch (203 mm) tiles.

Barnard, who joined in the late 1890s and contributed slip-decorated and other wares.

An enormous range of products was marketed for the delectation of the Victorian public, some of the designs being influenced by the displays seen at the great international exhibitions. The Japanese influence was very noticeable, and there were plaques of elegant women painted by Thomas Allen. Wedgwood made tiles from the 1870s. Despite all this, by the end of the nineteenth century the firm seems to have lost its way. It was Kennard Wedgwood (great grandson of Josiah II and grandson of Francis) who brought about a rationalisation of the range, discontinuing uneconomic products like tiles and expensive ornaments.

Frank Wedgwood joined the firm in 1888, becoming a partner in 1891. The firm became a limited liability company in 1895, with Cecil, Kennard and Frank as directors. Cecil was killed in 1915 during the First World War and Frank took over as chairman and managing director.

Arnold Austin, modeller at Etruria from 1904 to 1934, working on a lidded tureen in the 'Edmé' form. John Goodwin was responsible for the original design. The full range was developed between 1908 and 1912. Arnold Austin continued to work for Wedgwood until 1947.

THE TWENTIETH CENTURY

A showroom was opened in Paris in 1901, and an agent was appointed in the United States, where Kennard Wedgwood went in 1906 to establish a branch in New York to market Wedgwood in America.

John Goodwin became art director in 1904. He discontinued many

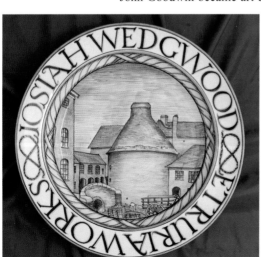

of the Victorian tableware designs but restored some earlier ones, conscious that Wedgwood's reputation rested on its eighteenth-century ranges. He realised that for a firm of this standing originality was hard to sell, despite the admiration of the design pundits. The Edmé shape on classical lines, designed by Goodwin around 1908 and which continues to sell well, proves this point.

Artwares were subsidiary to the basic business of tableware production. Lustre and freehand painted artwares were designed and produced by Alfred and Louise Powell. In 1911 Daisy

Round earthenware plaque with a view inside the Etruria Works, decorated by Alfred Powell (1865–1960). Diameter 482 mm. Impressed mark WEDGWOOD *and date mark for 1923.*

33

Bone china bowls c.1920–5 decorated with designs from the Fairyland Lustre range. 'Poplars' pattern. Printed mark WEDGWOOD *with the Portland Vase symbol and various other marks.*

Makeig-Jones was promoted from trainee paintress to the design staff. Two years later she produced the first of her lustre patterns on powder blue and in 1915 she introduced Fairyland Lustre, which remained popular for about fifteen years. Most patterns were withdrawn by 1931.

Wedgwood did not escape the effects of the collapse of the American economy in 1929. A further blow was the death of Frank Wedgwood in 1930. Goodwin retired in 1934 and was succeeded by Victor Skellern. Millicent Taplin, who had started in 1917 and was another important staff designer, retired in 1962. Skellern worked closely with Norman Wilson and Keith Murray, the architect, and he encouraged freelance designers to do work for Wedgwood. Among these were Eric Ravilious, Robert Goodden, Richard Guyatt, Rex and Laurence Whistler, Edward Bawden, John Skeaping, Doris Lindner, Arnold Machin and Eric Olsen.

Bone china teaware decorated with the 'Charnwood' pattern, produced by Wedgwood in 1944 and the first lithographically printed multicoloured transfer design. Printed mark WEDGWOOD *with the Portland Vase symbol and various other marks.*

34

Queen's Ware coffee set in matt white 'Moonstone' glaze, with knobs and handles trimmed with platinum, c.1935. Designed by Keith Murray. Height of coffee pot 203 mm. Impressed mark WEDGWOOD MADE IN ENGLAND *and, printed in blue,* KM. WEDGWOOD MADE IN ENGLAND. *Pattern number (in red) CH6099.*

By 1936 the Etruria Works was no longer suitable for modern manufacturing. Very considerable subsidence had caused the factory to sink 8 feet (2.4 metres) below the level of the canal. Much of the Etruria estate had been sold years before and the nearby Shelton Iron and Steel Company caused massive pollution problems. It was decided

Group of bone china ware featuring the 'Black Colonnade' pattern. The design has its origins in the early twentieth century and has been produced in black as well as gold versions. The name 'Colonnade' means a row of columns, especially those supporting an entablature or a roof. Marks various.

Group of items designed by Eric Ravilious (1903–42): (from left) Queen's Ware pedestal cup, 'Boat Race Day', c.1938, height 254 mm; handled mug, earthenware with black glaze, gold print of the 'Alphabet' design, which appeared first in 1937; earthenware Liverpool-shape jug with handled beaker, printed with 'Garden Implements' pattern designed by Ravilious in c.1938. Marks WEDGWOOD *impressed and printed, with various other marks.*

to move to Barlaston, where an all-electric manufactory was built with a model village close by. Although building began in 1938, the Second World War delayed its completion, and it was not until 1950 that all departments were accommodated in the new works. The Etruria Works was demolished in 1966, leaving only the round house as a reminder.

The Honourable Josiah Wedgwood, of the fifth generation, who had guided the firm for more than thirty-four years, was succeeded as managing director by Arthur Bryan in 1964 and as chairman in 1967. Sir John Wedgwood retired in 1966. They were the last two members of the family to hold senior positions in the company, which went public in 1967.

A programme of expansion by acquisition was started in 1966 and continued until the 1980s. The company became known as the Wedgwood Group in the 1970s. In 1986 the Wedgwood Group was bought by Waterford Crystal.

FURTHER READING

Atterbury, P. (editor). *The Parian Phenomenon*. Dennis, 1989.

Batkin, M. *Wedgwood Ceramics 1846–1959*. Dennis, 1982.

Bergesen, V. *Majolica*. Barrie & Jenkins, 1989.

Buten, D. *18th-Century Wedgwood. A Guide for Collectors and Connoisseurs*. Main Street Press, 1980.

Edwards, D. *Black Basalt. Wedgwood and Contemporary Manufacturers*. Antique Collectors' Club, 1994.

des Fontaines, U. *Wedgwood Fairyland Lustre*. Sotheby, 1975.

Dolan, B. *Josiah Wedgwood: Entrepreneur to the Enlightenment*. Harper Collins, 2004.

Karmason, M. G., and Stack, J. B. *Majolica. A Complete History and Illustrated Survey*. Harry N. Abrams, New York, 1989.

Kelly, A. *The Story of Wedgwood*. Faber & Faber, 1975.

Kemp, R. V. *George Stubbs and the Wedgwood Connection*. Published privately, Stoke-on-Trent, 1986.

Luedders, A. (editor). *Wedgwood. Its Competitors and Imitators 1800–1830*. Ars Ceramica, New York, 1977.

Mankowitz, W. *The Portland Vase and the Wedgwood Copies*. Deutsch, 1952.

Meteyard, E. *The Life of Josiah Wedgwood*. Hurst & Blackett, reprinted 1980.

Reilly, R. *Wedgwood*. Macmillan, 1989.

Reilly, R. *Josiah Wedgwood*. Macmillan, 1992.

Reilly, R. *Wedgwood. The New Illustrated Dictionary*. Antique Collectors' Club, 1995.

Shaw, S. *History of the Staffordshire Potteries*. 1829; reprinted by Scott, Greenwood, 1900.

Tames, R. *Josiah Wedgwood*. Shire, second edition 1984; reprinted 2001.

Uglow, J. *The Lunar Men. The Friends Who Made the Future*. Faber & Faber, 2002.

Wedgwood, B. and H. *The Wedgwood Circle 1730–1897*. Studio Vista, 1980.

Williams, P. *Wedgwood, A Collector's Guide*. Apple Press, 1992.

Wills, G. *Wedgwood*. Country Life, 1988; reprinted Spring Books, 1988.

Young, H. (editor). *The Genius of Wedgwood*. Victoria and Albert Museum, 1995.

PLACES TO VISIT

Old Wedgwood ware can be seen at the following museums but intending visitors are advised to find out the times of opening before travelling and also to ascertain that relevant items will be on display.

The British Museum, Great Russell Street, London WC1B 3DG. Telephone: 020 7323 8000. Website: www.thebritishmuseum.ac.uk

Broadlands, Romsey, Hampshire SO51 9ZD. Telephone: 01794 505010. Website: www.broadlands.net

Castle Museum, The Castle, Nottingham NG1 6EL. Telephone: 0115 915 3700. Website: www.nottinghamcity.gov.uk The Felix Joseph Collection.

Lady Lever Art Gallery, Port Sunlight Village, Bebington, Wirral CH62 5EQ. Telephone: 0151 478 4136. Website: www.liverpoolmuseums.org.uk

Liverpool Museum, William Brown Street, Liverpool L3 8EN. Telephone: 0151 478 4399. Website: www.liverpoolmuseums.org.uk

Manchester City Art Galleries, Mosley Street, Manchester M2 3JL. Telephone: 0161 235 8888. Website: www.manchestergalleries.org

The Manchester Museum, University of Manchester, Oxford Road, Manchester M13 9PL. Telephone: 0161 275 2634. Website: www.museum.man.ac.uk

The Potteries Museum and Art Gallery, Bethesda Street, Hanley, Stoke-on-Trent, Staffordshire ST1 3DW. Telephone: 01782 232323. Website: www.stoke.gov.uk

Salisbury and South Wiltshire Museum, The King's House, 65 The Close, Salisbury, Wiltshire SP1 2EN. Telephone: 01722 332151. Website: www.salisburymuseum.org.uk The Brixie Jarvis Collection.

Victoria and Albert Museum, Cromwell Road, South Kensington, London SW7 2RL. Telephone: 020 7942 2000. Website: www.vam.ac.uk

Wedgwood Museum, Josiah Wedgwood & Sons Ltd, Barlaston, Stoke-on-Trent, Staffordshire ST12 9ES. Telephone: 01782 282818. Website: www.wedgwoodmuseum.org.uk (Museum is currently closed for redevelopment and is expected to reopen in 2006)

UNITED STATES OF AMERICA

Birmingham Museum of Art, Oscar Wells Memorial Building, 2000 8th Avenue North, Birmingham, Alabama 35203-2278. Website: www.artsbma.org The Dwight and Lucille Beeson Collection.

Nassau County Museum, One Museum Drive, Roslyn Harbor, New York 11576. Website: www.nassaumuseum.com

AUSTRALIA

The Art Gallery, Melbourne, Victoria.

Powerhouse Museum, Museum of Applied Arts and Sciences, 500 Harris Street Ultimo, PO Box K346, Haymarket, Sydney, New South Wales 1238. Website: www.powerhousemuseum.com

MARKS

Earliest impressed marks c.1759–69

WEDGWOOD

Printed mark on bone china (and rarely on Queen's Ware) 1878–1900. ENGLAND was added from 1891 to comply with the McKinley Tariff Act of the USA for all imported goods

Impressed on useful wares 1769–80 and on all wares from 1780

WEDGWOOD

Earliest marks of the Wedgwood & Bentley partnership, used on ornamental wares only from 1769

Later version of the Portland Vase printed mark used from 1900; BONE CHINA was added from about 1937

WEDGWOOD

Seen on the plinths of Black Basalt vases, it is impressed or embossed on a circular disc of clay which has been applied to the plinth, 1769–80

Modern mark on bone china from 1962

WEDGWOOD
Bone China
MADE IN ENGLAND

Impressed mark varying in size and used on all types of wares 1780–95

edgwood.

WEDGWOOD
MADE IN
ENGLAND
ETRURIA

Printed mark on Queen's Ware from 1940 when the manufactory was moved from Etruria to Barlaston

Printed mark on stone china c.1820–61

)GWOOD'S
NE CHINA

WEDGWOOD
ENGLAND 1759

Mark introduced in 1998 for bone china and Queen's Ware

A selection of Wedgwood marks often seen. A larger range of marks may be seen in 'Wedgwood, A Collector's Guide', by Peter Williams, Apple Press, 1992.

ACKNOWLEDGEMENTS
The author thanks Gaye Blake Roberts and Pat Halfpenny and, most especially, Lynn Miller, for their great help in editing the text and supplying the captions to the photographs of their treasures generously provided by the Trustees of the Wedgwood Museum, Barlaston, Staffordshire. He also wishes to thank the many friends who have permitted him to photograph items in their collections and have assisted him in his study of Josiah Wedgwood and his wares, in particular Dr A. M. Kanter, the late Dr J. Whieldon, Mrs E. Chellis, Dean Rockwell, the late Harry Buten and the late Dr and Mrs Leonard Rakow. The author also thanks Kevin Salt for providing a CD-ROM of the images.
Illustrations are reproduced by courtesy of Josiah Wedgwood & Sons Ltd, except the following: page 4 (top), City Museum and Art Gallery, Stoke-on-Trent; page 5 (bottom), St Louis Art Museum; page 22 (right), Colonial Williamsburg; and pages 18 (both), 25, 27 (lower two), which are by the author. The cover photograph and illustrations on pages 18 (bottom) and 23 were taken by the author and are acknowledged to the Wedgwood Museum Trust. The map on page 9 is by Robert Dizon.

INDEX